The Life of
Moses

Written By CAROLYN MAGNER

Illustrated By ANNE KENNEDY

Chariot Books™
David C. Cook Publishing Co.

How to use My Bible Sticker Storybook

There are empty spaces in the pictures of each story. Lots of objects can be added to this picture. Find stickers of these objects at the back of the book to place wherever you like in the picture. The stickers are grouped by pages to help you choose the ones that go with the story.

This 1994 edition created and manufactured for Chariot Books by arrangement with
Ottenheimer Publishers, Inc.
Copyright © 1994 Ottenheimer Publishers, Inc.
10 Church Lane Baltimore, Maryland 21208
SF-819A
Printed in Hong Kong.

Contents

The Baby in a Basket

Exodus 1—2:10

Pharaoh was the cruel king of Egypt. He worried that the Israelites would become too powerful, so Pharaoh made the Israelites his slaves. He forced them to work long hours in the fields.

God blessed the Israelites with many children. Angry Pharaoh ordered that every Israelite baby boy be thrown into the river.

One Israelite mother hid her baby son, Moses, until he was three months old. She knew that the soldiers would eventually find him. So she made a basket from the reeds and hid him at the river's edge. The baby's sister, Miriam, hid nearby to make sure he was safe.

Pharaoh's daughter came to bathe in the river. She found the crying baby. "What a precious child," she said. "I will adopt him as my son."

Moses Hides from Pharaoh

Exodus 2:11-25

As a young man, Moses saw an Egyptian beating an Israelite slave. Moses became so angry, he killed the Egyptian and hid the body in the sand. When Pharaoh heard of this, he ordered that Moses be punished.

Moses fled to Midian, where he became a shepherd. One day, the daughters of a priest came to the well to get water for their thirsty animals. As Moses watched, mean shepherds tried to keep the women from the water. But Moses drove the shepherds away.

The daughters told their father, Jethro, about the kind stranger. Jethro invited Moses to stay with them. Soon, Moses fell in love with Zipporah, Jethro's daughter. He married her and they began a new family.

Back in Egypt, the Pharaoh had died. But the new king made the Israelites work even harder than before. They cried out to God for help. He heard their cries.

The Burning Bush

Exodus 3

One day, Moses stood watching his sheep near the mountain of God. Suddenly, Moses saw flames coming from a bush, but the bush did not burn.

Then God called from the bush, "Moses! Moses! Take off your sandals! You are standing on holy ground.

"I am the God of your fathers," God said. "I have heard My people crying for help. I will free them from slavery and lead them to a land of milk and honey.

"First, you must go to Pharaoh and plead with him to let the people go. The children of Israel will listen to you and follow you out of Egypt."

"How can I go before Pharaoh?" Moses asked.

"I will be with you," God answered.

Let My People Go

Exodus 5:1—6:12

Moses and his brother Aaron went to Pharaoh to deliver God's message. "The Lord our God says, 'Let My people go,'" Moses cried.

"I do not know your God," replied Pharaoh. "Why should I obey Him? Who does He think He is to give me orders?"

Pharaoh was so angry that he made the Israelites work harder.

Moses was sad. The plan was not working.

God told Moses, "I am the Lord, your God. Pharaoh will let My people go. I will show him many acts of My power, and I will free My people from slavery."

The Ten Plagues

Exodus 7:14—10:29

One morning, Moses and Pharaoh stood on the riverbank. "Pharaoh, you say you do not know the Lord," Moses said. "I will show you His power and you will let the people go."

Moses hit the river water with his staff. Instantly, the water turned to blood. All the fish died. No one could drink the water. But Pharaoh would not free the Israelites.

One week later, God sent a plague of frogs to change Pharaoh's mind. There were frogs in the palace, frogs in Pharaoh's kitchen, and frogs in his bed! Still, Pharaoh ignored God's warnings.

Next, God sent plagues of pesky gnats, swarms of flies, locusts, disease, hailstorms and darkness. In all, the Lord sent nine plagues, each one more horrible than the last.

Then, God promised the stubborn Pharaoh one more powerful sign.

The People Leave Egypt

Exodus 11—14

God told Moses that He would send one more plague to make Pharaoh let the people go.

At midnight, the firstborn son in every Egyptian home died. Even Pharaoh's own son died. But none of the Israelites died because they had obeyed God's word. They had taken the blood of a lamb and brushed it on the sides of the doorposts of their houses.

The next morning, the country was filled with the cries of Egyptian families. "Get out!" Pharaoh screamed at Moses. "Take your people and leave Egypt forever!"

The Israelites gathered all their belongings and left. But Pharaoh quickly changed his mind. He ordered his army to chase the Israelites and capture them.

The Israelites fled from the army until they reached the Red Sea. Now what should they do? They were afraid. The army was behind them, the sea was before them.

God instructed Moses, "Raise your staff and divide the water." The water parted and the Israelites crossed a dry path to safety.

14

The Ten Commandments

Exodus 19—20

Moses and his people camped at the base of a great mountain in the wilderness of Sinai. God called Moses to the top of the mountain to give him a message for the people.

"You have seen what I did for you in Egypt," God said. "If you obey Me and keep My laws, then you will be My special people."

God wrote his laws on two stone tablets. These laws are the Ten Commandments:

"You shall not worship other gods."

"You shall not worship statues or idols."

"You shall not misuse the name of the Lord."

"Remember the Sabbath day and keep it holy."

"Honor your father and your mother."

"You shall not kill."

"Husbands and wives should honor their marriage vows."

"You shall not steal."

"You shall not tell lies about your neighbor."

"You should not desire things that belong to others."

Moses stayed on the mountain listening to God's instructions for forty days and nights.

The Golden Calf

Exodus 32

The people grew tired waiting for Moses while he was on the mountain. "Moses brought us into the desert and then left us," they complained.

They decided to create a new god. "Let's melt our gold and shape it into the form of a calf!" they cheered.

When Moses came down from the mountain with the Ten Commandments from God, he saw the people dancing around the golden calf. Moses became so angry that he smashed the stone tablets on the ground. Then he destroyed the golden calf.

Once again, Moses went before the Lord. "Please forgive the people for this great sin. If you cannot forgive them, destroy me instead," Moses pleaded.

"I will forgive them," God said. "Now go and lead My people."

Moses returned to the people carrying God's blessing, and two new stone tablets.

Forty Years in the Wilderness

Numbers 14

God had promised Moses and the Israelites freedom in a land rich with fruit, fertile soil, and flowing water. Moses sent twelve men into the land of Canaan to check out the land. When they returned, ten men reported that the land was indeed very rich. However, the people were fierce and as big as giants!

The other two men were Joshua and Caleb. They agreed with the other men, but declared, "We can take the land. God will help us!"

But the people were afraid and doubted God's promise. They grumbled, "We will never get to the land of milk and honey."

"Because the people do not trust Me, they must remain in the wilderness for forty years," God proclaimed to Moses. "Only their children and Joshua and Caleb will go into Canaan."

For forty years, the Israelites wandered in the wilderness. They learned how to work together and to trust God. They grew tough and strong from the many trials and battles they faced on their journey. But only their children would one day enter the Promised Land.

The Death of Moses

Deuteronomy 34

When Moses was an old man and ready to die, God sent him to the top of a mountain overlooking the beautiful land of Canaan. "This is the land I have promised My people," God told Moses. "There was a time that you doubted Me. Because of this, you cannot lead them into Canaan."

After gazing into the distance at the Promised Land one last time, Moses died.

The Israelites were sad to lose their courageous leader. They would always remember the gentle man who freed them and taught them to trust the Lord. No other man has shown the awesome power of God to Israel as Moses did.